Comfort Cow and Friends

A book of skills to help with emotional regulation

COLORING PAGES INCLUDED!

Carly Schoonover, LCPC

Illustrations by Blueberry Illustrations

ISBN-9798849989686

Comfort Cow and Friends

A book of skills to help with emotional regulation

Disclaimer: The purpose of *Comfort Cow and Friends* is to help people develop skills and tools that can help with processing and regulating difficult emotions.

I am a Licensed Clinical Professional Counselor and I teach these skills to my clients. The information provided in this book is not intended to be a substitute for professional medical advice, diagnosis, or treatment that can be provided by your own physician, nurse practitioner, physician assistant, therapist, counselor, mental health practitioner, licensed dietitian or nutritionist, or any other licensed or registered healthcare professional.

Do not use our content in lieu of professional advice given by qualified medical or mental health professionals and do not disregard professional medical or mental health advice or delay seeking professional advice because of information you have read in this book.

If you are in crisis or you think you may have an emergency, call your doctor or 911 immediately.

If you're having suicidal thoughts, call 988 (National Suicide Prevention Lifeline) to talk to a skilled and trained counselor at a crisis center in your area at any time. If you are located outside the United States, call your local emergency line immediately.

Dedication

This book is dedicated to all humans out there who are struggling. You are not alone. We are all in this together, and we can change the world if we all treat each other with kindness and grace.

To all my clients, your strength has inspired and continues to inspire me to be a better person and therapist.

To my husband, children, parents, and brother. You all have changed me in ways that you will never know. Your love for me gives me purpose and my love for you keeps me going. Thank you for accepting all the parts of me.

To my lifelong friend Emily, who has played an important part in the creation of this book. I asked Emily to be my partner in this because I trust her judgment and talent. This book wouldn't be what it is without her involvement in it.

Emily has helped assist in perfecting the writing, illustration placement, and character development. I am lucky to have such a wonderful and talented friend in my life.

This book belongs to

....

My name is Logan and I don't know what people think of me and I am worried. My tummy hurts and my hands are clammy, my thoughts are scurried.

Scary thoughts fill my mind and my fear just grows. I know that all this fear buildup definitely shows.

I am struggling to shower and eat my food. I am feeling yucky and just can't seem to shake this bad mood.

Can you help me out? I don't know what to do with all this doubt.

Hi Logan, I am the Comfort Cow and I'm here to help. Your mind is racing and your thoughts are moving fast. I am going to help you slow down, this doesn't have to last.

Take a deep breath, breathe in 1-2-3-4-5 and out 1-2-3-4-5-6-7-8. Try it again, this time connecting with the feeling of the air moving in and moving out; you can do this practice, I have no doubt.

Slowing down your breathing can help to soothe your nerves and bring on a more relaxed state. At the same time, name your emotions. That's it, you are doing great!

Keep in mind that not every thought is the complete and total truth. Once you start to become aware of your thoughts, you will start to notice the proof!

One thing that is for sure, we don't know what others are thinking. Put your attention back on your fear, do you notice it shrinking?

If not, that's OK, checking in is key. What are your thoughts doing right now, can you check in and see?

Take each thought that enters your mind and place it on a cloud. This helps to give you and your thoughts some space, so they aren't so loud.

Watch each thought float on by, but don't rush them along. Allow them to float at their own pace and you might notice, the thoughts don't feel so strong.

Practice makes progress, give yourself time and space. The first step will always be slowing down your breathing, that skill is your base.

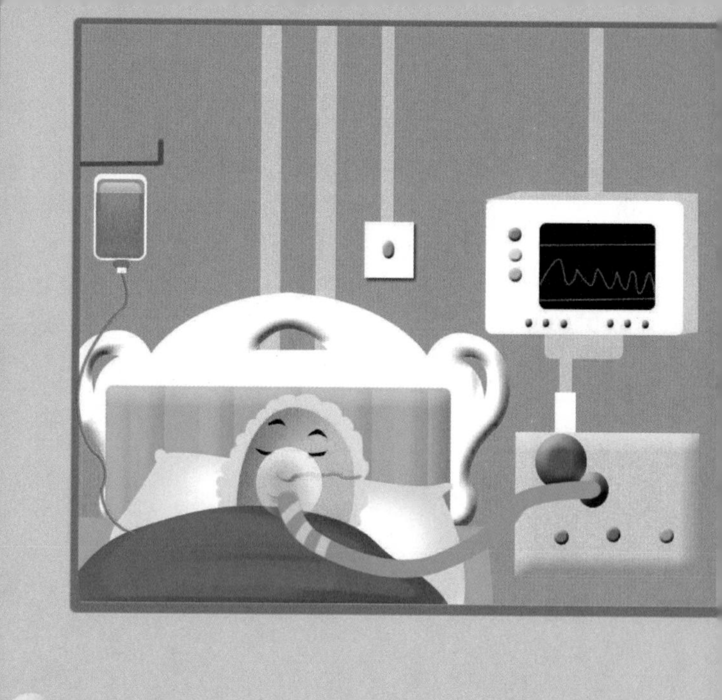

HOSPITAL
ICU →

My name is Avery. My grandma is sick and I am feeling scared. I don't want her to die, I am not prepared.

I don't know what to do, my stomach is in a knot. My heart is tense and heavy, and I am scared to cry, because it will be a lot.

I just want to feel happy, I don't like feeling scared and sad. It's hard to tell, but I think I am also feeling mad!

Can you help me please? I am hoping I can feel more at ease.

Hi Avery! I am the Comfort Cow and I'm here to help. It is hard when things aren't in our control. It can feel scary and unsettling, and feeling it is the goal.

"Name it to tame it," let's do that one first. Start with the feeling that feels as though it may burst.

Nice job naming them, you did so well! Allow yourself to feel, but there is no need to dwell.

When we avoid our feelings, they get trapped inside. We can't escape our feelings, we can't run and we can't hide.

Our emotions are like waves in the ocean. Sometimes the waves are calm and other times they are more rough and can create quite a commotion.

Allow the wave (emotion) to complete, it has a beginning, a middle, and an end. Allowing your emotions to do their thing can be a new and healthy trend!

Ride the wave by accepting how you feel. Take some deep breaths and push your feet in the ground. Stomp your feet down, and hear the sound.

Care about your emotions, they are here to protect you. Emotions aren't here to make you miserable, I promise that this is true.

No matter how big the feeling, you are always bigger than it. Practice makes progress and no matter what, just don't quit.

The way through is accepting the feeling, that is the way to start the healing.

My name is Anthony. It's hard to sit still in class and focus or learn new things. I get nervous because I am not sure what today brings. I want to stay home with my family where I feel safe; my fear of separation stings.

It's hard not to know, my brain thinks of the worst. My heart beats so fast, I fear it might burst!

What if I say something wrong or someone makes fun of me? It makes me feel anxious, like I just want to run and flee!

Can you help me figure it out so I can start to feel happy? I hope you can do it and that it can be done snappy!

Hi Anthony! I am the Comfort Cow and I'm here to help. It is hard to sit with uncertainty around us, but I can help you cope, that's what we will discuss.

First, close your eyes and take in a deep breath 1-2-3-4-5. Blow it out real slow 1-2-3-4-5-6-7-8. Slowing down your breathing can help you to think more straight.

Our brain likes to know what is happening, so when we don't, that can feel like a threat. Shifting your thoughts to "Hey, I can handle it" will be your most helpful asset.

We can easily overestimate the threat and underestimate our ability to handle it, and I think that's what is happening here. You are more capable than you think, so there is no need for all this fear.

Think about a time when you were unsure. You figured it out and handled it, keeping this in mind can help you to feel more secure.

IT IS OK
TO BE AFRAID

I CAN DO
HARD THINGS!

I AM
UNIQUE AND SPECIALI

I AM
LIKEABLE AND LOVED

" I WILL FEEL "LONELY

" I CANT DO THIS"

" NOBODY WILL LIKE ME "

What are your strengths? Tell them aloud to me... Wow, you do have a lot! Remembering these will be another key.

Use your strengths to help you get through uncertainty and to create change. It might feel weird at first, a little bit strange.

Don't believe everything you think, for each thought is not a fact! This may help you notice them and name them, so they don't have as much impact.

Another helpful tip is to put your thoughts on a leaf and let it float down a stream. This helps create distance between you and your thoughts, this skill and you can be a great team!

Believe in yourself, and remember your strengths. This will help you in great lengths.

You are capable of handling what comes your way, keeping this in mind will help keep your fears away.

My name is Molly. Nobody wants to play with me and I don't know why. I go by the kids I used to play with and they run from me, and I want to cry.

I feel sad and hurt that my friends have left me alone, they have ditched me to play all on my own!

Why don't they like me, what is wrong? I haven't been friends with them for so long.

I don't want to play all by myself, I want to be included! But I am not. Instead, I am being excluded.

I am not sure what else I can do. I wish I could figure it out, I wish I only knew.

Hi Molly! I am the Comfort Cow and I'm here to help. I can tell you are feeling hurt and sad. You want to play with your friends again, you want to really bad.

First and foremost, take a deep breath in, and a deep breath out real slow. OK, let's see what is going on and just so you know, from this experience, you will grow.

Be the type of friend that you would want for your own. Think about this for a bit, to make it more known.

OK, so you want friends who are kind, nice, and caring? And also friends who don't have a problem with sharing?

Treat others as you want to be treated. Be kind, nice, and caring and you can't lose, you won't feel defeated.

The right friends will want to be friends with you too. Stop trying so hard and be open to them, let them come to you.

I am sorry you feel so lonely right now. That loneliness is helping you move toward others and can help you make new friends, as long as it's something you will allow.

You are quite likable, we all are in our own way. The right people will notice and the right people will stay.

Let's talk about how you can find new friends today. Let me help you, I will show you the way.

Think about hobbies, what you like to do. Give it some thought, think it all the way through.

Art, music, and dance, you say? There are many who like them too, let's find a club or group today!

Joining activities will help you connect with others and make new friends. Be open to new people; on you, that depends.

Practice an open posture, which will signal to people, "Hey, I am open to talk!" With this approach, the right friends will flock.

How do I practice an open posture, you ask? Spine straight, head up, don't cross your arms, it's not too much of a task.

Put a smile on your face, even if it's half; it feels good to smile and feels good to laugh!

Now that you know, let's get started. You will find your friends, I say this wholehearted.

You got this, I know it to be true. You will find what you are looking for, you will find your friend crew!

My name is Adelia. I feel sad and it's hard to get out of bed. I can't think straight and can't get out of my head.

My eyes are heavy and my chest is tight. I know that I just don't feel right.

It's hard to think about the future and I have little hope. All I feel like doing is being by myself so I can mope.

I have stayed away from doing anything fun. It feels like too much effort to move and I fear nothing can be done.

Can you help me feel better please? This depression has brought me to my knees.

Hi Adelia! I am the Comfort Cow and I'm here to help. Oh, I am sorry you are feeling this way. It seems you have lost yourself, you have gone astray.

Let me help you get out of this depression trap, I will help you disrupt this pattern and that will be a wrap!

First and foremost, this is not your fault. Sometimes these feelings come on and they can feel like an assault.

The first step is to be aware and ask for support. So hooray to you, for this depression, together, we will abort!

As always, let's first take a deep breath in, letting the air fill your lungs. And now let it out, and let's wiggle our tongues!

That was silly and it helped bring upon a smile. That smile looks good on you, it's definitely your style!

When we smile, our brain sends chemicals that help to relieve stress. Then what do you think will happen to your sadness, can you take a guess?

It won't feel so bad because your smile is helping you out, and you are taking action that is opposite of a pout!

So smile, even if you feel sad. I can't promise that this will help completely, but it will definitely help a tad!

So smile all you can! Watch a funny movie or tell a joke, make this part of your coping plan.

Depression feels heavy and urges us to lay in our bed all day and sleep. Let's take a different action, one that involves moving your body. I know that may feel like a big leap.

Open your shades and turn on a light. This alerts your brain that it's time to wake up, it's no longer night.

Eat some breakfast to get started with your day; then do something to fill your soul, maybe meditate or pray.

It's helpful to plan your day out, it keeps us more structured and less filled with doubt.

Move your body and get your daily tasks done. Also, make sure you are doing things that involve fun!

Talk with others that you trust, express how you feel. It's good to confide in others, it really is ideal.

Explore and connect with values that matter to you. Make choices that align with your values, in all that you do.

Let's put the finishing touches on this plan. Get enough quality sleep as much as you can.

Do things that you feel confident doing. Think about your talents, those are worth pursuing.

You say you like drawing and writing and think you are good at both? Recognizing your talent is already a sign of your growth!

Draw or write at least once a day. Connecting with what comes natural helps to lift the gray.

We have a plan, are you ready to try? You are so brave and I am proud of you, your limit is the sky!

My name is Mitchell. I feel mad easily and then I act out. I slam doors, kick the walls, and scream and shout!

I get in trouble and then I feel bad, I never mean to get so mad. I sit in my room and feel very sad.

I don't want to shout, I don't want to destroy my things. All it does is get me in trouble with my parents, that's all it brings.

Then I feel bad and wish I didn't hurt people with the words I said. I wish I could figure it out, and just make nicer choices instead.

Please help me control what I do and say when I am feeling this rush of rage. I can't continue to get mad and then start a rampage.

Hi Mitchell! I am the Comfort Cow and I'm here to help. It's OK to feel angry, the problem is not what we feel. It's what we do with the emotion, it's our actions and how we deal.

Feeling mad and then being aggressive is not the way to cope. This can damage our relationships and then we start to lose even more hope.

Let me help you manage this anger in a more effective way. It involves being more in control of your body, and keeping these unhelpful actions at bay.

I want you to feel your feelings and express them in a way that is healthy and more steady. You are asking how to do that, and I think you are ready.

The first step is to notice what your body feels like when you are starting to feel upset. Does your heart race, do your fists clench, do you start to sweat?

When we can notice our anger before mean words come out, then we can be more intentional with what we say and we can control our urge to shout.

You control your body, not your feelings of rage. When you notice these intense sensations, then helpful skills you can start to engage.

Notice how your body feels when you start to feel irate. With intention, slow down your breathing and this skill will help you stay in control without it being too late.

Now take a step back from the situation, give yourself space to slow down. This will keep you in control of your body, in your anger you won't drown.

In this space, slow your breathing and maybe count to 10. Or you can write your feelings in a journal, you just must grab a pen.

Now notice what is happening. What is the situation and what are your thoughts doing? Being aware of what is happening outside and inside of you will keep your anger from further brewing.

Our thoughts can fuel our anger until it feels out of control. So be aware of what you are thinking, this will keep those thoughts from going down an angry rabbit hole.

Remember, you are not your thoughts and when we are angry, our thoughts are often not true. Being aware will keep those angry thoughts from continuing to accrue.

Another skill is to move your body safely to release all that energy that anger can bring.

Do some jumping jacks, push-ups, run in place, feel free to choose your own active thing!

The very last thing to remember is to consider which actions to take that are filled with respect.

Do you need to talk about your feelings to a loved one, do you need to connect?

Choose your behavior, your anger doesn't have to run the show. When you practice these actions, your abilities will continue to grow.

Now that you have a plan, are you ready to put it into action? Once you get started, you will start to gain traction.

It won't always be easy, but with practice, you will improve. Remember, anger gives us lots of energy, so don't forget to move!

HOSPITAL
ICU →

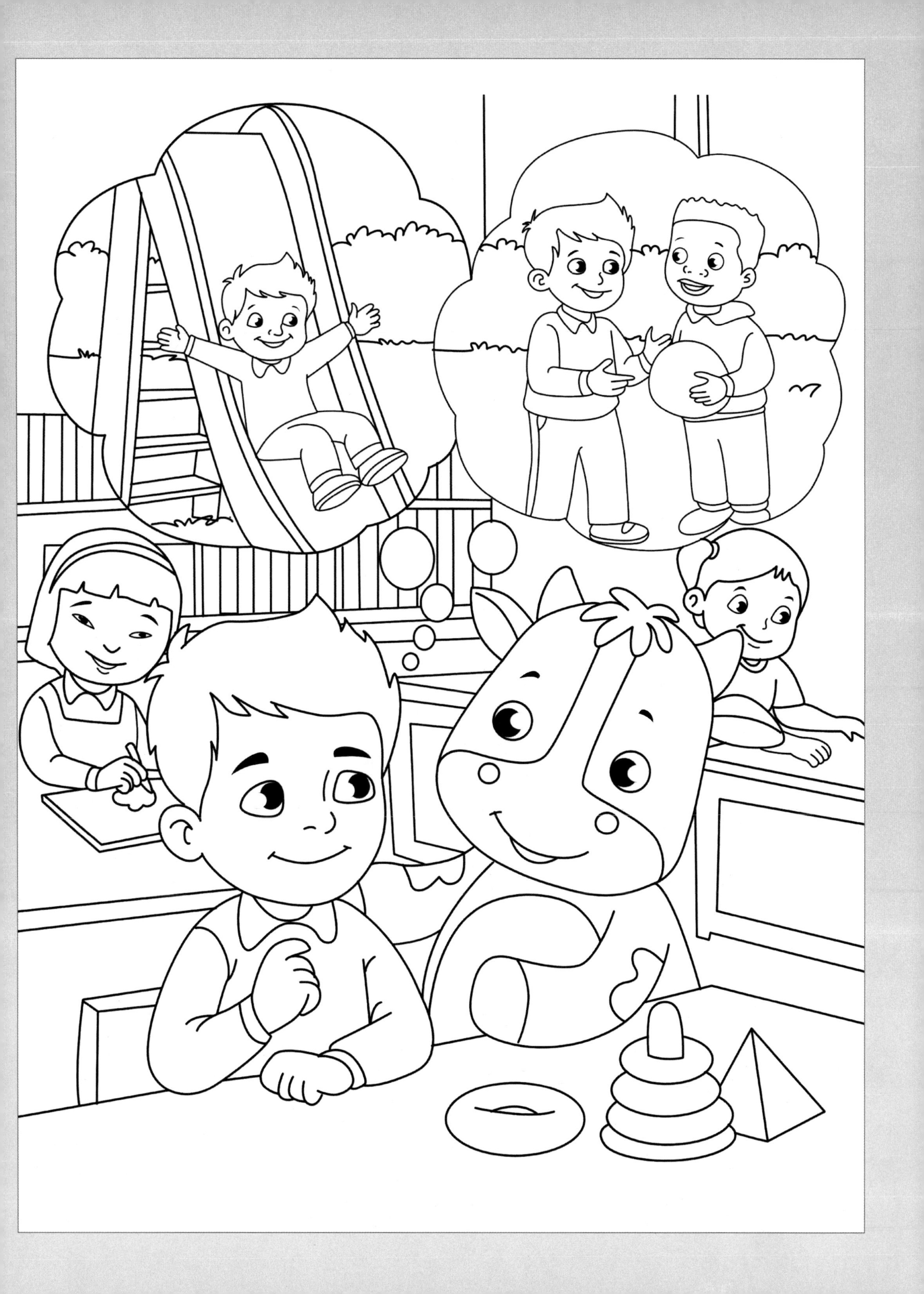

IT IS OK
TO BE AFRAID
I CAN DO
HARD THINGS!
I AM
UNIQUE AND SPECIALI
I AM
LIKEABLE AND LOVED
" I WILL PEEL "LONELY
" I CANT DO THIS"
" NOBODY WILL LIKE ME "

About the Author

Carly Schoonover, LCPC is a practicing therapist and a mother of two beautiful children. Her amazing clients and her own children have inspired her to write this book, which offers challenging, real-life scenarios in combination with practical and scientifically proven ways to help cope with difficult emotions.

Carly is on a mission to share these useful tools and skills with the world. Carly's main passions in life are her family, helping others, learning, being in nature, and at the root of it all, experiencing life fully, in the present moment.

Carly lives in Crystal Lake, Illinois, with her two children, husband, two dogs, a cat, two turtles, and lots of fish!

Emily LeBeau is a wife and a mother of two children with a background in design and a passion for psychology. She has been inspired by her own experiences as a child and a parent which have been benefited by a gentle and supportive approach using scientifically proven tactics and exercises.

Paired with a fervent desire to share these tools and knowledge base with others, she is honored to help bring *Comfort Cow and Friends* to life.

Emily lives in Pingree Grove, Illinois, with her loving husband, two wonderful children, and a dog. Her interests include DIY projects, reading, watching movies, making quality memories with family and friends, and ultimately learning to slow down and live life purposefully.

Made in the USA
Monee, IL
18 October 2022